Nish Dubashia

The Unity of Everything

Everything

A Conversation with David Bohm

Copyright © 2018 Nish Dubashia

Publisher: tredition, Hamburg, Germany

ISBN
Paperback: 978-3-7439-9299-3
Hardcover: 978-3-7439-9300-6
eBook: 978-3-7439-9301-3

I dedicate this book to

David King
for his tireless work over decades
as we together explored
and tried to make sense
of the human mystical experience

Adi Da
for showing me
that all historical traditions
are just branches
of the One Great Tradition

and to Shilpa
for travelling with me
and always supporting me
on this strange journey
that we call our life

CONTENTS

Prologue

Introduction

Epilogue

Appendix

Bibliography

In some sense man is a microcosm of the universe; therefore what man is, is a clue to the universe. We are enfolded in the universe.

- David Bohm

PROLOGUE

In 1984, while a Mathematics student at Warwick University, I began to seriously practice Buddhist meditation under the guidance of various Buddhist monks who would periodically visit the university, a practice that would continue unabated for the next thirty-four years.

At this time, I also discovered the writings of the Indian mystic Jiddu Krishnamurti, whose teachings bore a strong resemblance to what I was learning and experiencing as a Buddhist. Krishnamurti's descriptions of what he referred to as "choiceless awareness" mirrored almost exactly the techniques of Buddhist meditation (vipassana and zazen) that I was practicing.

"Observe, and in that observation there is neither the "observer" nor the "observed" — there is only observation taking place." - Jiddu Krishnamurti ("Fear and Pleasure", The Collected Works, Vol. X)

As a student of Applied Mathematics, I had a basic familiarity with the concepts of quantum mechanics, and I began to notice certain similarities between some of the findings of quantum physics and some of the insights and teachings of Mahayana Buddhism, the school of Buddhism to which I was the most attracted.

For example:

""*All matter originates and exists only by virtue of a force... We must assume behind this force the existence of a conscious and intelligent Mind. This Mind is the matrix of all matter.*""

— Max Planck (Originator of Quantum Theory)

Soon after this, I discovered the writings of David Bohm, one of the greatest living physicists and quantum theorists, who was developing a theory of reality in which, like Krishnamurti had already asserted, the observer and the observed were deeply interconnected, and like in Mahayana Buddhism, the whole of the manifest universe emerges or arises out of a deeper order of reality or wholeness in which both consciousness and matter find their common ground.

"In the enfolded [or implicate] order, space and time are no longer the dominant factors determining the relationships of dependence or independence of different elements. Rather, an entirely different sort of basic connection of elements is possible, from which our ordinary notions of space and time, along with those of separately existent material particles, are abstracted as forms derived from the deeper order. These ordinary notions in fact appear in what is called the "explicate" or "unfolded" order, which is a special and distinguished form contained within

the general totality of all the implicate orders" – David
Bohm, Wholeness and the Implicate Order. p. xv.

David Bohm has been described as one of most
significant theoretical physicists of the 20th century.
Bohm worked for many years as a professor at Princeton
University, where he worked closely with Albert
Einstein. In addition to physics, Bohm became deeply
interested in the nature of consciousness and the role of
thought in creating human conflict. His work in this area
was developed even further as a result of his friendship
and subsequent interactions with the Indian mystic
Krishnamurti, in whose teachings Bohm saw insights
quite compatible with those he was developing in
quantum physics.

Based on my study of Eastern mysticism and Western
Neoplatonism, I was already developing my own model
of how mystics see reality. In this model, the whole of
reality emerges out of a primordial non-dual Ground or
Source of All Things. This Wholeness of Reality is then
split into two by the action of human awareness, which
creates a dualism between the observer and the
observed in its perception and experience. Out of this
twoness emerges the entire world of multiplicity, of
separate things and events in space-time. And when we
take this multiplicity too far, and create parts of the
whole that are not really separate or separable (such as
human races or religions) we create fragmentation,

which leads to a crisis in perception and violence and division in the world.

The spiritual quest could be seen as the reversing of this process of descent whereby the Ground ends up being fragmented in human consciousness, by means of a process of ascent whereby fragmentation, then multiplicity, then dualism, and finally even wholeness are healed and returned to their Source as Ground in human enlightenment.

The process of descent could thus be seen as consisting of essentially five levels or stages:

1. The Ground of All Being, the Source of All Things.
2. The Whole of Reality, seen as a Boundless Unity.
3. The Primary Dualism: Observer vs. Observed.
4. Multiplicity: Things-Events separated in Space-Time.
5. Fragmentation: Illusion as Multiplicity goes too far

In reverse, the process of ascent could be seen as consisting of four essential stages:

1. The ordering of thought, fragmentation is

healed
2. Profound awareness of how we create sense of self
3. The healing of the self-other dualism in Unity
4. Going beyond even Unity itself, back to the Ground

Once I was reasonably confident that this model had something useful to say, I wrote a paper describing the model, explaining the different levels or stages in more detail, and showing the extraordinary correspondences that seemed to exist between this model and the models of reality described by many different philosophical and spiritual traditions throughout history.

I then, rather audaciously, sent the paper to David Bohm at Birkbeck College in London, confidently expecting never to hear from him.

To my astonishing surprise, I received a phone call at home from Dr. Bohm a couple of months later inviting me to meet him at his London office to discuss some of the ideas in my paper in more detail.

What follows is the transcript of our discussion.

I dedicate this transcript to my friend David King for his tireless work over decades as we together explored and tried to make coherent and intellectually defensible sense of the human mystical experience.

And I cannot thank the late Dr David Bohm, one of greatest scientists of the twentieth century, enough for sparing a couple of hours of his valuable time to speak with me, an ordinary and relatively insignificant Buddhist meditator and student of mysticism. He is deeply missed.

- **NISH DUBASHIA**

INTRODUCTION

A DIALOGUE WITH DAVID BOHM

This dialogue took place on 10th January 1991 at Birkbeck College, London. The model discussed and referred to is produced below for reference, and is in the form it took from May 1990. It has since been substantially revised, in part from insights gained during this meeting.

THE MODEL:

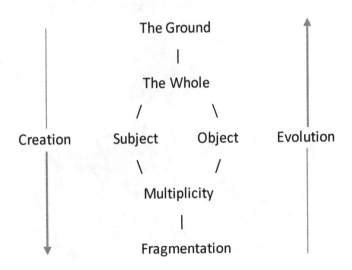

THE MODEL APPLIED TO THE WORK OF DAVID BOHM:

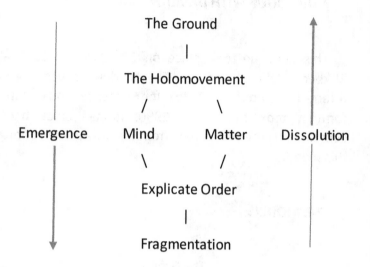

THE MODEL APPLIED TO THE PHILOSOPHY OF KRISHNAMURTI:

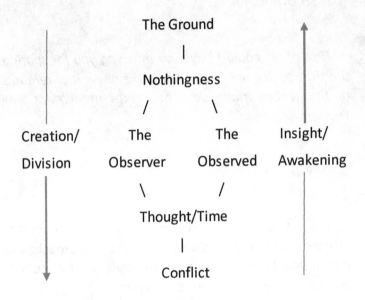

PART ONE: THE PART AND THE FRAGMENT

NISH DUBASHIA:

First of all, could I begin by thanking you for sparing the time to see us? Could you make any initial remarks on the general model described in the manuscript that I've sent you?

DAVID BOHM:

Well, you seem to have developed a coherent scheme, and you've shown that all these approaches fit into your scheme. Many such attempts are incoherent, but yours seems to be quite coherent.

DUBASHIA:

A good way to proceed with this discussion may be to look at each component of the model separately, and also look at how they relate to each other. The distinction at the bottom between multiplicity and fragmentation is very much one that I have derived from your own work. To put it another way, the two levels represent the distinction between the part and the fragment. Could you perhaps say something about this distinction? Can we make it clear what this distinction is?

BOHM:

Well, parts are parts of a whole, whereas fragments are just arbitrary divisions that are not related to each other or to the whole. Parts of a machine all fit together, but if you smash it you would produce fragments. When thought creates abstractions which have been carried too far because of fragmentation, it takes the abstraction as the thing itself. Things that are not separate are treated as separate. They are not really parts. Like the fragmentation between countries. People come to believe that the boundaries between countries really exist, and say "This is my country." But these countries all depend on each other.

One can take a similar attitude to the organs of a body.

All such abstractions should be made with a 'dotted line' so that we don't take them too seriously. Instead we draw a solid line, and fragmentation arises. The thought process takes itself too literally.

DUBASHIA:

So, can we say that the distinction between a part and a fragment is not just in the division itself, but in our attitude to that division?

BOHM:

Yes. We have a fragmentary attitude. To distinguish a part makes sense if the divisions are natural in some way. We know that such natural divisions exist in nature, right? But if we take something that is not materially broken into parts, and say that it is broken into parts, then those parts lose their connection to the whole and we have introduced an incoherent way of thinking and acting in relation to the whole. Thought just smashes things up. People are guided by fragmentary thought when they smash things up.

DUBASHIA:

The distinction between the part and the fragment – is that analogous in some way to Krishnamurti's distinction between technological and psychological thought?

BOHM:

Well, in a way. You could say technological thought divides correctly to produce parts, whereas psychological thought divides what is undivided. It 'pretends' to divide. Like dividing the observer from the observed.

PART TWO: THE OBSERVER AND THE OBSERVED

DUBASHIA:

The distinction between the observer and the observed – are you saying that that is a fragmentation?

BOHM:

Yes. It's a distinction that is taken too far. It's not only taken as a distinction but as a separation or a division. That's the way psychological thought works. It treats the parts as separate. When the observer and the observed are seen to be different, then one can act on the other. But in fact they are not different, so the attempt of one to act on the other is false.

The so-called observer – his very being arises from the observed, right? So, if he wants to observe anger, his whole way of operating is affected by the anger that he wants to observe. There is no 'me' that can observe the anger objectively, right? Thought actually attributes itself to the things it wants to observe. Say for example you are watching television, and you see a telephone on the screen; it appears to be actually there. You perceive it to be there. Thought affects the perception. According to how thought attributes it, that's the way you perceive it. So thought can attribute falsely and you then perceive falsely.

Thought separates the observer from the observed as a concept. It attributes observation to the observer and attributes itself to the observed. So it creates an image of the observer looking at the observed. It mistakes its perception for reality. Thought then says that the observer wants to look at the observed, but in order to look the observer should not be conditioned by the observed. Any stray emotion interferes. The observer is compelled to observe, but it is observing according to the emotions, not according to the reality. So, the observer is not independent of the observed, and the observed is not independent of the observer, because the way you think determines the way you observe. So there is no way to divide them. They are simply figures of the human mind, to which is attributed reality. If we attribute reality, then the way we experience reality is not real.

DUBASHIA:

The difference between the observer and the observed is, in a certain sense, necessary or functional.

BOHM:

Where there is a relative separation. So, you see, with regard to external matter, in most cases there is some separation, so the connection is weak and therefore the observer is not conditioned too much by what he observes, and the observed is not conditioned by the observer. Therefore, that model is a good approximation, but not perfect since there is still some connection. But when applied to the mind, that model is totally incoherent. It can become incoherent outwardly too, since the way you think affects the way you observe. What you're seeing may not be real, since your attitude affects the way you perceive things. You'll see things according to your conditioning. You see, self-deception can occur technologically too, but at least technology can avoid it. But it cannot be avoided if the observer and the observed are separated absolutely.

DUBASHIA:

You also make the distinction between the self and the ego. Could we say that the self exists as a result of the distinction between the observer and the observed when it is seen to be relative, whereas with the ego the division has spilled into areas where it is not valid?

BOHM:

If the distinction between the observer and the observed is kept within its proper limits then there is no problem. But, but when it is not kept within those proper limits then it spreads into the ego. You see, thought can attribute to itself all sorts of qualities and try to defend these, even if they are not right.

But there's another view of the self which is that the self is unknown — this is the ancient view. The self is unknown because we are dealing with something that has nothing to do with the observer or the observed. Whatever it is, it is unknown.

DUBASHIA:

Many of the mystical traditions have said that the distinction between the subject and the object is, in some sense, the primary distinction that is made. It's that division which is then extrapolated to generate the whole spectrum of multiplicity.

BOHM:

There is also a division between thought and reality. In some sense thought is part of reality – thought is part of the physical body – but we tend to divide it, as if thought were a purely spiritual principle independent of the body. That implies the division between the observer and the observed.

The thought process comes along and says it's separate, but that's incoherent, you see – the division between the thinker and the thought. One may think that the thinker is a purely spiritual entity but, you see, the thinker **is** the thought, and the thought is part of the body. The whole process is of the body. But that is very much against most of our culture. Thought is a very subtle material process. You cannot separate it.

Every part affects the whole, and the whole affects every part. Thought, assuming that its source is a pure unconditioned entity, will not see that. It will treat itself as true, and also as some separate entity which, on the basis of truth, can act on all things.

DUBASHIA:

In some sense, that division is the source of fragmentation.

BOHM:

Yes. That's the first fragmentation, it would seem. This division between thought and reality, between thought and what you're thinking about. That division works very well in certain areas – that's the whole point. But it's extended to the whole, right?

DUBASHIA:

This is what I've tried to represent in my model, with the division between the subject and the object.

BOHM:

Now the ground must include not only the whole but the parts, you see.

DUBASHIA:

Yes.

PART THREE: THE GROUND OF ALL BEING

BOHM:

If you say that the ground is just the whole, then that's already a fragmentation.

DUBASHIA:

Yes. This is the main reason why I've separated the ground from the whole in my model. Many people seem to feel that the whole is the ultimate, but the whole is in fact one half of a dualism since it is opposed to the part.

BOHM:

It's opposed to multiplicity. The ground must include both the whole and multiplicity.

DUBASHIA:

You talk in 'The Ending of Time' with Krishnamurti about the particular dying to the universal, and the universal also dying to the ground. Could you elaborate on that?

BOHM:

You can see that the particular originates in the universal – the universal particularizes itself. Now, maybe we should go back, you see. The whole movement is one of the particular emerging from the universal. And this particular eventually dies away. Now, the universal has no meaning without the particular. Therefore, Krishnamurti suggested that even the universal, the thought of the universal – which is a kind of fragmentation – has to die into the ground. Because the thought of the universal implies the multiplicity which is necessary for its meaning. In any case, if all the particulars were to vanish, the universal would vanish too.

DUBASHIA:

So, by the ground, one is referring to a perception that includes both the universal and the particular in a greater unity.

BOHM:

Yes. Some people have tried to understand it by thought, but it cannot be represented. We can say that there is a form of 'seeing' that is coherent. But most of us seem to operate in fragmentation, and with fragmentary thought you get results that you don't intend or want, you see. So, for example, people created nations for all sorts of purposes, but out of that fragmentation they get results that they don't want, like war and destruction.

PART FOUR: CREATION AND EVOLUTION

DUBASHIA:

I've suggested, in my scheme or model, that the way the different components interact is by a process of creation or evolution. Could you perhaps say something about that?

BOHM:

Well, I don't know what to say. Perhaps you should explain what you mean by that.

DUBASHIA:

You've spoken about the way in which the different parts that we perceive emerge, in some way, out of the whole. Now, in a sense, those parts are being created. If we look at evolution as a process whereby there is a general movement towards greater order and greater wholeness, then in a sense it is the reverse of the process of creation. Various spiritual traditions, for example, have talked about the whole evolution of man as a movement towards, ultimately, a perception of the ground.

BOHM:

Well, the first movement is towards unfoldment and multiplicity. And multiplicity comes back to the whole.

DUBASHIA:

The movement of multiplicity back to unity — is it correct to call that evolution?

BOHM:

Well, you can call it that, yes. The movement of multiplicity back to wholeness results in some kind of higher development — it doesn't just go back to what it was.

DUBASHIA:

Could you explain that?

BOHM:

Well, we're not going to simply make a circular movement – out to multiplicity and returning to wholeness. It's more like a   spiral. It comes back on another level. That's the view of evolution, right? Evolution would be the whole movement by which the movement out to multiplicity and back to wholeness together move onto a higher level.

DUBASHIA:

Right. So in a sense the whole level itself is evolving.

BOHM:

Yes. Now, at this higher level, it may turn out that one has, in some way, touched the ground, you see. That would be a creative act of coming back together as a whole. One could say that the movement of multiplicity is a necessary step.

DUBASHIA:

Why?

BOHM:

Well, as part of the creativity. It's a two-way movement. The whole and the part are not really separated – they are only separated when you bring in time.

DUBASHIA:

Right. So the whole and the part are evolving together.

BOHM:

Yes.

PART FIVE: MIND AND MATTER

DUBASHIA:

As you can see from my thesis, I've suggested equivalent formulations of the general model for various traditions. Could we have a look at the one that I have suggested in relation to your own work? Do you have any general comments?

BOHM:

Right. Well, the holomovement splits into mind and matter which together generate the explicate order.

DUBASHIA:

Could you say something about how mind and matter together generate the explicate order? This is not entirely clear.

BOHM:

Well, we didn't see also how the subject and object generate multiplicity. We must ask the question of how that occurs. The division of subject and object is necessary for multiplicity. In fact, it already **is** multiplicity. So how does that get to multiplicity? Do you have an answer for that?

DUBASHIA:

Well, I would suggest that the initial split is the division between the thinker and the thought. Then that process of division continues, extrapolates and generates more and more divisions. Then what you get is a world of different objects. In a sense it's the same process continuing. There is a saying in Taoism, for example, that the one becomes the two, and the two becomes the many.

BOHM:

Well, it's not clear here why the two becomes the many. How is it so? How does two become three, you see? There is a subject and an object, right? The subject is observing the object. The subject divides the object.

So the object changes to reflect the subject. So in some way they are multiplying, but it's not quite clear.

You see, the way I see it is that you start with the whole. The whole just simply becomes multiplicity. I haven't explained how it does it. You're trying to explain it.

DUBASHIA:

I'm trying to suggest an intermediary stage by suggesting that this is the first split.

BOHM:

Yes.

DUBASHIA:

I'm basing that, first of all, on my understanding of the mystical traditions I've mentioned, that talk about the 'Primary Dualism'.

BOHM:

Well, one can see that people will split the object according to the needs of the subject. And the reason the object is divided is that the subject must do something with it.

DUBASHIA:

So, can we say that before you can come to a perception of multiplicity you need a sense of an observer separate from the observed?

BOHM:

Yes. The observer is there in order to do something, you see. This division is necessary whenever you want to do something. What you do will require that you divide the object. The only way that this could proceed would be to divide the object.

DUBASHIA:

Right. So there's never really a stage where there is just two.

BOHM:

No.

DUBASHIA:

It's a bit of an abstraction to say that.

BOHM:

Yes. Because the subject begins to act on the object and begins to divide the object. That division is either coherent or not — technologically it's coherent and psychologically it's not. In fact, very often, technologically it's not.

DUBASHIA:

What I'm trying to suggest is that the level of 'Subject vs. Object' being placed 'higher' than the level of multiplicity is really suggesting that it is this entity — the 'self' — that then proceeds to divide. It's not strictly accurate in the sense that it does not proceed historically in that order.

BOHM:

No

DUBASHIA:

There isn't a stage where there is just an object out there as one unity.

BOHM:

No. Well, the subject will actually keep on dividing. You see, if you are experiencing the world as one object, then that means you are perceiving the whole.

DUBASHIA:

Right. There wouldn't be a subject in such a perception.

BOHM:

No.

DUBASHIA:

Right. So it's really an abstraction.

BOHM:

Yes.

DUBASHIA:

*What I'm trying to convey is that the realm of multiplicity is generated by thinking. So I'm just suggesting that this thinker and thought division has to be present there in **some** sense. Multiplicity is then extended beyond its present limits to produce fragmentation. That's what I'm trying to convey.*

BOHM:

Right. Well, if the subject has certain needs, there must be distinctions made in the object to satisfy those needs. In the ground, the fact that you are dividing using thought and that thought works up to a point is clearly perceived. But we carry it too far.

DUBASHIA:

Right.

BOHM:

You would have to say that the holomovement splits into two 'sides': mind and matter. Mind being considered as different to matter will produce the same divisions according to the needs of mind.

PART SIX: KRISHNAMURTI

DUBASHIA:

If we turn to the next page, I've suggested an equivalent model for the teachings of Krishnamurti. I've derived this very much from the 'Ending of Time' where he talks about 'no-thing' ness.

BOHM:

Yes. The holomovement.

DUBASHIA:

And again, we have multiplicity being related to thought and time, and that gets carried on too far to spill over into psychological thought and time. And I've suggested that by the awakening of intelligence one can come to a perception of the ground – the whole can be seen as fragmentation dissolves.

BOHM:

Yes. I can see what you're saying. But, of course, Krishnamurti felt that was only the beginning, and that the ground was much more than this.

DUBASHIA:

Can you explain that?

BOHM:

Well, he didn't say too much about it, but simply that for people to whom this was happening there would open up endless possibilities for discovery and transformation. That would not simply mean the ending of our troubles.

DUBASHIA:

That's just the first step.

BOHM:

Yes.

PART SEVEN: EVOLUTION AND TRANSFORMATION

DUBASHIA:

I've attempted to relate this model to the question of what a human being can actually do in his attempt to understand the movement of thought and bring the mind to a state of silence. Therefore, in addition to these various equivalent versions of the general model, I've also attempted to use this model to understand the awakening of intelligence. So, if we can turn please to section 8 of my thesis.

Again, it's an equivalent model, but here I've presented it from the point of view of what man can actually do to bring some kind of clarity to each of these 'levels'.

So perhaps if we can start from the bottom of this model and work up.

BOHM:

Yes.

DUBASHIA:

At the bottom, we have fragmentation. Moving up to the level of multiplicity, what I'm suggesting is that this relates to what Krishnamurti referred to as 'laying the foundation' or what you yourself have called 'bringing order to the field of measure'. Now that would belong to the realm of multiplicity.

BOHM:

Yes.

DUBASHIA:

You're not actually going beyond multiplicity, but you are bringing a great deal of clarity and energy to that area. It's a necessary foundation before you can move onto self-observation and meditation.

BOHM:

Yes. That's right.

DUBASHIA:

Then, at the level of subject-object, I've suggested that the process of attention, awareness and meditation would really belong there. Because what you're doing is observing the movement of the self.

BOHM:

Yes. And you have to be aware that the subject and the object are really one, right?

DUBASHIA:

Yes.

BOHM:

Now, once you're aware that they are one, you would change. You can see that the movement is incoherent. Once you have perceived that thought is incoherent fully, then that stops. The real perception of that incoherence. We are perceiving it now through inference. Intellectual inference has its place. But by means of a direct perception thought will be aware of its own movement. When this thing is directly perceived this movement of incoherence will stop. The body will no longer go on with it.

Now, thought being part of the body will also not go on. So, thought will then stop operating except where needed, where it can work coherently.

DUBASHIA:

One subject that has never clearly been resolved for me is the question of this process whereby thought observes itself and looks at the way it is creating conflict – that observation, is that deliberate?

BOHM:

Yes. That's a paradox. If it's too deliberate then you have an end and a means, then you are separating, you are projecting the end to be achieved with the means. The observer will have produced the very thing that you want to get rid of, right?

Now there is something you can do. You see, time cannot come in. Because time is the means of projecting the end in the future and trying to reach it. You're here, it's there. The observer is here, the observed is there. Is there a movement, then without time, you see? That doesn't mean that the clock is not working. We're talking about psychological time.

Now we're conditioned in this time. So the pervasive conditioning is the system, or systemic thought. So one part of the system tries to look at the other part. Now what Krishnamurti is saying is that if, without trying to do anything, if we're interested, if we begin to see this thing, then it will work. It may not work immediately because we are so conditioned in so many ways, so that we may see it in parts, and in parts we don't see it. So, we don't just have to work on the outward order, but on the inward order – watching the disorder in thought and feeling and trying to see how they are related.

Now, thought can attribute itself to anything. It attributes itself, and this affects how you perceive things. That is the fundamental mistake. As long as it does that it will inevitably bring in time. So, how are we going to stop doing this?

DUBASHIA:

Now Krishnamurti says that the 'how' is the wrong question.

BOHM:

But that's a paradox, you see.

DUBASHIA:

That's right, yes.

BOHM:

Now, in the case of the body, we have the perception we want. When you move your arm, you know immediately that it's you who's done it, right? You don't have to stop it moving through time. If you imagined that it was somebody else who was moving it, you could fight it.

Such a perception is necessary for the survival of the body. Thought being part of the body should be capable of such a perception. There's a movement of thought, a movement that creates thought, which we don't see. Thought cannot be aware of itself because it can think only of its content. The whole movement of thought can be aware of itself, just like the body can be aware of itself. So we can suggest that it is possible for the whole movement of thought to be aware of itself at the very moment that it is moving — not to be aware by inference, since inference cannot do it. That would create the division of the observer and the observed.

DUBASHIA:

This awareness arises naturally when one has an interest.

BOHM:

When one has enough interest so that one is not caught up in conditioning. If something is very important to you, then this conditioning drops, right? If your life is in danger, you suddenly find that you are very alert since all the things that occupied your mind have suddenly been dropped.

DUBASHIA:

Krishnamurti has suggested that this awareness, if carried out with sufficient clarity and intensity, will lead to a state of psychological silence where the observer is the observed.

BOHM:

It will simply remove the illusion that the observer is not the observed.

DUBASHIA:

In the same way that we said earlier that the whole and the part are two halves of a dualism that are transcended by the ground, could we also say that the state of silence and the state of thought are two halves of an analogous dualism?

BOHM:

Well, I don't know. You could say that possibly. The ground must include all of that. Thought must take its place, although it may be a much smaller part than thought imagined.

DUBASHIA:

It simply assumes its rightful place.

BOHM:

Yes.

PART EIGHT: THE TRANSFORMED BEING

DUBASHIA:

Krishnamurti talks about the transformed or enlightened human being. Because such a person has in some way contacted or had a perception of the ground which transcends the whole and the part, the state of his own mind will have transcended the division between thought and no-thought, each of which assume their rightful place. Could you say something about that?

BOHM:

Well, there's not much to say. The orderly functioning of the mind would lead thought to take its rightful place. All of our current confusion disrupts the brain, makes life hazardous. The perception of the way this occurs would make the mind silent. Another way of looking at this is that we have to become aware of the now. At present we are in the future and the past. The future and the past are really taking place **now** in the mind, right? But they are being projected and assumed to be in different places, as if the future were ahead and the past behind.

Now, when we are thinking about it, rather than contacting it, we are separating the observer and the observed by the introduction of time, and we are not in the now. The thinking process is in the now but the content is not. There also feelings which are induced by thought. Every thought will induce a feeling. Feelings are closer in contact with the now. The point is that when awareness goes to those feelings, usually it's avoiding them – it's conditioned to avoid the feeling that you are disturbed. But if you can stay with them with awareness through all that, then you can begin to see thoughts coming in which are responding to the feelings, which are trying to avoid the fact – such as "things will get better", "this is no good – I want it different." The judgements which condemn the present state which thought itself is producing, produce more and more conflict, and keep it all down. Perhaps if you can stay with that, then perhaps you could begin to see closer to the now. The feeling is now but thoughts suddenly come in. The feeling is trying to unfold, but they come in very fast and push them back. You can see that is happening. Now, if you could stay with that, awareness begins to come into it at that present moment. Now awareness of the present moment has got to be what transforms us because only the present moment is **what is**. Any transformation must come from what is happening in the present moment. The awareness has to be of the present moment. But thought is continually dealing with the past and the future, which are not there – although they are good approximations for practical purposes.

Fundamentally, time is not the essential order. Being in the now will make the observer-observed separation impossible.

DUBASHIA:

One of the points I was trying to bring out in my model is that transformation is not something separate from daily life.

BOHM:

No

DUBASHIA:

One contacts the ground, but that perception still has to be integrated into one's daily life. In that way, one sees that the ground is not only transcendent, but it is immanent as well. There is a notion in some traditions, such as Zen, that we are already enlightened.

BOHM:

Well, potentially. If we say that we are already enlightened, then it's not very clear why all these enlightened beings are creating so much confusion.

(Laughter)

DUBASHIA:

Yes

BOHM:

The potential is to remove the causes of unenlightenment. The potential is to remove the confusion, but it's not definite, right? Instead of seeing the truth that the observer is the observed, I have to remove the illusion that the observer is not the observed, the conditioning to that illusion. It's like a reflex. Also remove the illusion that I exist in time. One depends on the other. Once you remove the illusion that you exist in time, it becomes impossible to sustain the illusion that the observer is not the observed. The minute you say you exist in time, you must have that separation.

EPILOGUE

When my conversation with David Bohm came to a natural end, I thanked him for his time and generosity, and asked him what the next step should be for me in the development of my model. He replied:

"The next step would be to put it into practice, to live it."

I took his words seriously, and continued to devote myself to a rigorous practice of Buddhist meditation (primarily vipassana – the development of insight into the true nature of reality – and samatha – the calming of the mind through mindfulness of breath) for the next two decades.

In 2007, seventeen years later, this single-minded devotion to serious spiritual practice would begin to bear fruit, and I would spend almost six months in a state of extraordinary peace and equanimity. Thoughts would arise only a few times each day when needed for practical purposes or rare conversation. The sense of separate self would disappear and the absolute unity of all things would be obvious and self-evident. Both the unity and the diversity of all things would playfully arise in an Unconditioned Awareness which was seen to be the True Buddha-Nature of all sentient beings everywhere. The model of reality that I had discussed with David Bohm seventeen years earlier would come to life in, as and through me. And even though this realization would gradually reduce in intensity, I would remain eternally gratefully for this glimpse of enlightenment that I had been given.

- **NISH DUBASHIA**

APPENDIX

I.   THE MODEL APPLIED TO HINDUISM

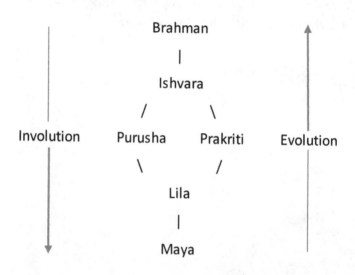

Brahman – the Ultimate Reality, which is both transcendent and immanent. The Supreme Cosmic Spirit.

Ishvara – the Oneness in everything and everyone. The monistic Universal Absolute. Sometimes personalized as the Supreme Being or Personal God.

Purusha – The self or consciousness.

Prakriti – Matter, the observed empirical reality.

The interaction between Purusha and Prakriti accounts for the universe of separate things, events and experiences.

Lila – The universe of separate things, events and experiences seen as the play of the Divine, as parts of a unified Whole.

Maya - The universe of separate things, events and experiences seen without any awareness of the Divine, as fragments without any awareness of the Whole.

II. THE MODEL APPLIED TO BUDDHISM (MAHAYANA)

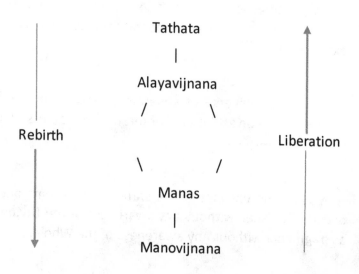

Tathata — the ultimate nature of reality, the way things really are, beyond conceptualization and description.

Alayavijnana — the 'storage consciousness' of the universe, which contains the seeds of all future manifestation, the impressions of all past existence and experience.

Manas – the thinking mind that divides the whole into different parts

Manovijnana – the division process is taken too far and existence is viewed dualistically. The parts become fragments and one becomes attached to the results of one's own thinking.

III.   THE MODEL APPLIED TO TAOISM

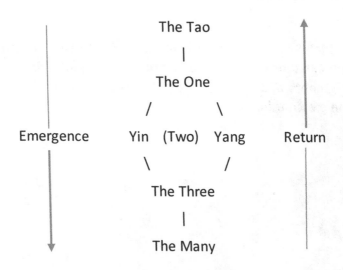

The Tao gives birth to One. One gives birth to Two. Two gives birth to Three. Three gives birth to all things.
-    *Tao Te Ching, Chapter 42*

The Tao – the order or essence of the Universe, present in both the One and the Many.

The One – the Whole, the interconnectedness and Oneness of everything, the great unification.

The great unification splits into the Primary Dualism.

Yin and Yang – the fundamental duality that lies at the origin of the world of multiplicity.

The Three – the great harmony in and of pluralism that arises when the Yin and the Yang interpenetrate each other.

The Many – the disharmony that arises when the balance is lost, and the world is no longer in harmony with the Tao.

IV.   THE MODEL APPLIED TO JUDAISM (KABBA-LAH)

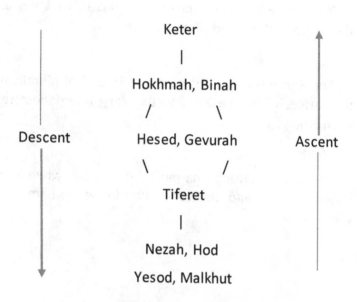

Keter – The Ground of All Being, encompassing both the wholeness of creation and all of its parts.

Hokhmah/Binah – Existence before multiplicity, the first point of true existence, contains within it the potential for multiplicity

Hesed/Gevurah – the right and left of existence, whose interaction creates the world

Tiferet – the world of beauty, with each part playing its role and being perfectly synthesized with every other part

Nezah, Hod, Yesod, Malkhut – obstacles arise, the separate self emerges, limited individuality is born, identification with the body becomes the norm

V.   THE MODEL APPLIED TO CHRISTIANITY

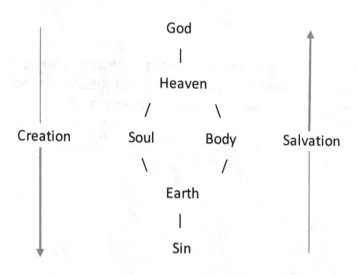

God – the Supreme Being, both transcendent and immanent

Heaven – the realm or state of perfect Wholeness

Soul – the immaterial consciousness within man/woman

Body – the material form of man/woman

Earth – the world of separate things and events, originally created in perfect harmony

Sin – the world when seen and experienced in a state of separation from God, a fallen world

VI.   THE MODEL APPLIED TO NEOPLATONISM

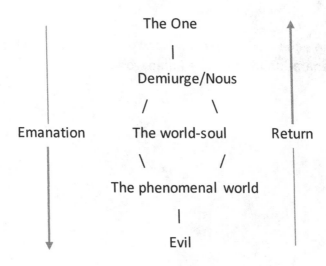

The One - the Creative Source and End of all things

Demiurge/Nous – the archetype of all things,
manifesting and organizing the world

The world-soul – stands between the nous and the
phenomenal world, embraces individuality

The phenomenal world – the world in unity and harmony

Evil – the replacement of unity and harmony with strife and discord, the absence of light and good

VII. THE MODEL APPLIED TO THE PHILOSOPHY OF KRISHNAMURTI

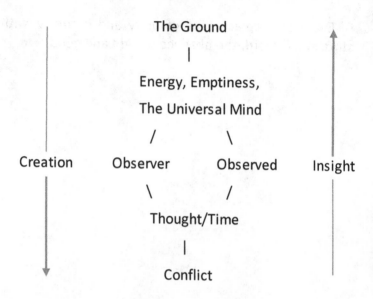

The Ground — The Absolute upon which everything exists, beyond energy, emptiness and silence, beyond even the universal. That beyond which there is nothing.

Energy, Emptiness, the Universal Mind — The cosmos, the whole, that which is completely beyond thought. That out of which nature and the particular arise.

The observer and the observed — Perception arises, and a relative and (at this stage) non-problematic division between the observer and the observed is made for purely practical and functional purposes.

Thought/Time – Conceptualization arises, as does the experience of chronological time.

Conflict – Conceptualization is carried over into areas where it is not appropriate, and psychological time is created. The observer experiences itself to be absolutely separate from the observed, and conflict arises, initially internally, and then externally.

VIII. THE MODEL APPLIED TO THE PHILOSOPHY OF KEN WILBER

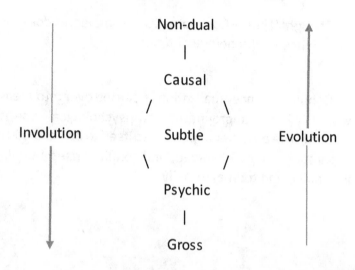

The gross realm – The sensorimotor world. Normally perceived in the waking state.

The psychic realm – Expansion of identity to embrace all of nature. Can give rise to clairvoyant perception and supra-sensory cognition. The realm of nature mysticism. The realm of the yogi and the shaman.

The subtle realm - Experience of deity forms and archetypal selves. Perception of Divine Light beyond nature and the cosmos. The realm of theistic mysticism. The realm of the saint.

The causal realm – Experience of the Abyss or the Void that lies beyond the Divine Light. Emptiness, the Divine Darkness, the True Self. The realm of monistic mysticism. The realm of the sage.

The non-dual realm – The perfect integration of Emptiness and Form. All manifestation is recognized as the play of Emptiness, as the play of one's True Self. The realm of full enlightenment. The realm of the adept.

IX.   THE MODEL APPLIED TO THE PHILOSOPHY OF AUROBINDO

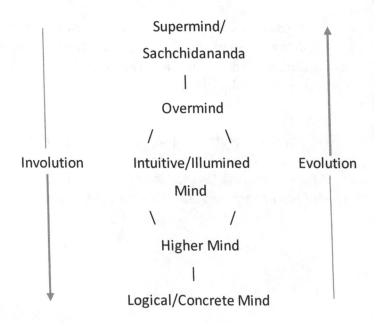

Supermind/
Sachchidananda
|
Overmind
/   \
Involution   Intuitive/Illumined   Evolution
Mind
\   /
Higher Mind
|
Logical/Concrete Mind

Logical/concrete mind – The mind thinks logically and forms concepts and opinions.

Higher mind – The first of the trans-rational levels of being. Sees the unity in the midst of diversity. Sees large aspects of the truth and a vast range of possibilities.

Illumined/intuitive mind – Beyond thought and into the spiritual light. Vision replaces thought. Subject and object penetrate, see and feel one another. Higher truths are remembered and seen.

Overmind – The original intensity out of which everything comes. The ground of the phenomenal world. The principles that causes multiplicity.

Supermind/Sachchidananda – Infinite and unitary truth and consciousness. Both transcendent and immanent. The Many in the One and the One in the Many. The Absolute and the Real.

X.   THE MODEL APPLIED TO THE WORK OF ADI DA

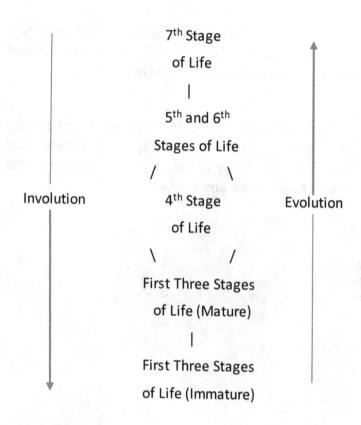

7th Stage
of Life
|
5th and 6th
Stages of Life
/   \
Involution   4th Stage   Evolution
of Life
\   /
First Three Stages
of Life (Mature)
|
First Three Stages
of Life (Immature)

First Three Stages of Life (Immature) – Dysfunction. Failures of adaptation. Chronic feelings of being separate and rejected. Adolescent dramatization.

First Three Stages of Life (Mature) — Healthy integration of body, emotion and mind. Mature adult. Fully autonomous human character.

4th Stage of Life — Divine Contemplation and devotion to God as Other or Supreme Object.

5th and 6th Stages of Life — Realization of the Divine Light (5th Stage) or the Transcendental Consciousness (6th Stage) that lies behind all of existence, but does not truly include or embrace that existence.

7th Stage of Life — The realization of the True Nature of everything. Every apparently separate "thing" is perfectly identical to God or Divine Consciousness.

RECOMMENDED READING

Da Love-Ananda, *Dawn Horse Testament*

Daniel Chanan Matt, *The Essential Kabbalah: The Heart of Jewish Mysticism*

David Bohm, *Wholeness and the Implicate Order*

Eva Wong, *Taoism: An Essential Guide*

Georg Feuerstein, *The Yoga Tradition: Its History, Literature, Philosophy and Practice*

Jiddu Krishnamurti, *Freedom from the Known*

Jiddu Krishnamurti and David Bohm, *The Ending of Time*

Ken Wilber, *The Religion of Tomorrow: A Vision for the Future of the Great Traditions — More Inclusive, More Comprehensive, More Complete*

Pailiina Remes, *Neoplatonism*

Paul Smith, *Integral Christianity: The Spirit's Call to Evolve*

Paul Williams, *Mahayana Buddhism: The Doctrinal Foundations*

Sri Aurobindo, *The Integral Yoga: Sri Aurobindo's Teaching & Method of Practice*

Though there are many historical traditions of religion and Spirituality, in Truth, there is one Great Tradition. . . . The Great Tradition of humankind is a universal tradition, because it is based on the One Reality — not only the Great, Indivisible Non-conditional Reality, but also the unity of conditional existence and the commonality and unity of human beings themselves.

Adi Da Samraj, The Ancient Walk-About Way

CPSIA information can be obtained
at www.ICGtesting.com
Printed in the USA
FSHW010542150321
79500FS